SMART SELLING

Harnessing AI for Marketing, Sales, and Service Success

Henry William

Henry William

Chapter 1:

Introduction to Smart Selling

Introduction:

In today's fast-paced and hyper-connected business landscape, organizations are constantly seeking innovative ways to stand out from the competition and drive success in their marketing, sales, and service efforts. One of the most transformative technologies making waves across these domains is Artificial Intelligence (AI). With its ability to process massive amounts of data, identify patterns, and make intelligent predictions, AI is revolutionizing how businesses engage with customers, personalize experiences, and drive revenue growth.

Welcome to the world of smart selling, where AI serves as a powerful ally in achieving marketing, sales, and service success. In this book, we will embark on an exciting journey, exploring the myriad ways in which AI can transform traditional business practices and help organizations gain a competitive edge.

From lead generation and personalized marketing strategies to sales performance management and customer service optimization, AI is reshaping the way businesses interact with their customers. With AI-powered tools and algorithms, companies can better understand customer needs, predict buying behaviors, and deliver targeted messaging and offers that resonate on a personal level. The result? Heightened customer engagement, increased conversion rates, and improved customer satisfaction.

But the impact of AI in smart selling goes far beyond personalized marketing. AI also enables sales teams to work smarter and more efficiently. From automating routine tasks and streamlining sales processes to providing real-time insights and recommendations, AI empowers sales professionals to focus on building relationships, solving complex problems, and delivering exceptional value to customers.

In this book, we will dive deep into the world of smart selling with AI. We will explore the latest trends and technologies, delve into real-world case studies, and provide practical guidance on integrating AI into your marketing, sales, and service operations. We will address the ethical considerations of using AI, the evolving roles and skills of sales professionals, and the future of smart selling.

So, whether you are a marketing executive looking to enhance customer engagement, a sales manager aiming to boost revenue, or a customer service leader striving to deliver exceptional experiences, this book is your roadmap to harnessing the power of AI for marketing, sales, and service success. Get ready to unlock new possibilities, drive growth, and take your organization to new heights in the era of smart selling. Let's embark on this exciting journey together!

1.1 The Evolution of Sales in the Digital Age:

This section explores the transformation of the sales landscape in the digital age. It discusses how advancements in technology and changing consumer behaviors have reshaped the way businesses sell their products or services.

It highlights the shift from traditional sales methods to digital sales channels and the increasing importance of leveraging technology to stay competitive.

1.2 The Role of Artificial Intelligence in Sales:

This section delves into the role of artificial intelligence (AI) in revolutionizing sales practices. It explains how AI technologies, such as machine learning and natural language processing, have enabled businesses to gain valuable insights, automate tasks, and enhance decision-making in sales.

It discusses how AI can augment the capabilities of sales teams by analyzing large amounts of data, providing personalized recommendations, and improving the overall efficiency and effectiveness of the sales process.

1.3 Benefits and Opportunities of Smart Selling:

This section outlines the benefits and opportunities that arise from adopting smart selling practices empowered by AI.
It explores how AI can help businesses better understand their customers, identify sales opportunities, optimize sales processes, and enhance customer experience.

It discusses the potential for increased sales productivity, improved sales forecasting accuracy, enhanced lead generation and qualification, and the ability to deliver personalized and targeted sales messages to customers.

It also addresses the potential challenges and risks associated with integrating AI into sales operations and provides an overview of the topics that will be covered in subsequent chapters.

The introduction chapter sets the stage for the book by providing an overview of the changing sales landscape, the role of AI in sales, and the benefits and opportunities of adopting smart selling practices. It aims to familiarize readers with the core concepts and motivations behind leveraging AI in sales and sets the foundation for the subsequent chapters that delve into the various aspects of smart selling empowered by AI.

Chapter 2:

Understanding AI in Sales

2.1 Fundamentals of Artificial Intelligence:

In this section, we provide readers with a solid understanding of the fundamentals of artificial intelligence (AI). We start by defining AI and exploring its key components. We introduce machine learning, which enables computers to learn and make predictions without explicit programming. Additionally, we discuss natural language processing, which enables computers to understand and interpret human language, and computer vision, which allows computers to perceive and interpret visual information.

We further delve into different types of machine learning algorithms, including supervised learning, unsupervised learning, and reinforcement learning. Supervised learning involves training a model with labeled data to make predictions or classifications. Unsupervised learning involves extracting patterns and insights from unlabeled data. Reinforcement learning involves training models through a reward-based system, allowing them to learn from trial and error.

2.2 AI Applications in Sales:

In this section, we explore the various applications of AI in the sales domain. We highlight how AI can enhance sales processes and enable more effective customer interactions.

Customer segmentation and targeting: AI can analyze large volumes of customer data, including demographics, behavior, and preferences, to segment customers into distinct groups. This allows businesses to tailor their marketing and sales strategies to specific customer segments and target them with personalized offers and messages.

Sales forecasting and predictive analytics: By leveraging historical sales data and market trends, AI algorithms can predict future sales patterns and identify potential opportunities or risks. Predictive analytics enables sales teams to make data-driven decisions and optimize their strategies for better sales performance.

Lead scoring and qualification: AI algorithms can automatically score and qualify leads based on predefined criteria and historical data analysis. This helps sales teams prioritize their efforts on leads that have a higher likelihood of conversion, improving efficiency and productivity.

Personalization and customer experience enhancement: AI enables personalized recommendations and tailored interactions with customers. By analyzing customer data and behavior patterns, AI algorithms can provide personalized product recommendations, content, and offers, enhancing the overall customer experience and increasing the likelihood of conversion.

Chatbots and virtual assistants in sales interactions: AI-powered chatbots and virtual assistants can handle customer inquiries, provide product information, and assist customers throughout their buying journey. They can offer instant support, answer frequently asked questions, and even make product recommendations, providing a seamless and efficient sales experience.

2.3 Machine Learning and Predictive Analytics for Sales:

In this section, we focus on the specific role of machine learning and predictive analytics in sales. We explain the basics of machine learning algorithms and their training process. This includes data preprocessing, feature selection, and model training. We emphasize the importance of high-quality, relevant data for accurate predictions.

We then discuss the application of predictive analytics in sales, showcasing how historical sales data, market trends, and external factors can be leveraged to make informed predictions and identify patterns. Predictive analytics enables sales teams to optimize sales strategies, allocate resources effectively, and identify potential upsell or cross-sell opportunities.

Lastly, we provide guidance on implementing machine learning models in sales processes. We discuss considerations such as model deployment, integration with existing sales systems, and ongoing model maintenance. We highlight the importance of continuous learning and adaptation to ensure the effectiveness and relevance of AI-driven sales solutions.

Overall, Chapter 2 provides readers with a comprehensive understanding of AI in sales. By exploring the fundamentals of AI, its applications in sales, and the role of machine learning and predictive analytics, readers gain the necessary knowledge to leverage AI effectively in their sales processes and drive improved sales performance and outcomes.

Chapter 3:

Building a Smart Sales Strategy

3.1 Setting Clear Sales Goals and Objectives:

- **Importance of setting clear sales goals:** This section highlights the significance of setting clear sales goals and objectives to drive the smart selling strategy. It emphasizes that goals provide direction, motivation, and focus for sales teams, enabling them to align their efforts with the overall business objectives.

- **Aligning sales goals with business objectives:** It discusses the process of aligning sales goals with the broader objectives of the organization. This alignment ensures that sales efforts contribute to the overall success and growth of the business.

- **SMART goals:** The section explores the concept of setting SMART goals - Specific, Measurable, Attainable, Relevant, and Time-bound. It provides guidelines for crafting goals that are clear, quantifiable, achievable, relevant to the sales function, and have specific timelines for accomplishment.

- **Data-driven goal setting:** It explores how AI can assist in goal setting by analyzing historical sales data, market trends, and customer insights. AI can provide data-driven recommendations and insights to help sales teams set realistic and ambitious sales targets.

3.2 Identifying Target Customers and Segments:

- **Understanding customer needs and preferences:** This section emphasizes the importance of understanding customer needs, preferences, and buying behaviors. It discusses the significance of gathering customer insights through various means, such as market research, customer surveys, and data analysis.

- **Customer segmentation:** It explores the concept of customer segmentation and its role in tailoring sales strategies and messages. The section explains how businesses can divide their customer base into distinct segments based on demographic, psychographic, or behavioral characteristics.

- **AI-driven customer segmentation:** The section delves into how AI technologies can contribute to customer segmentation. It discusses how AI can analyze large volumes of customer data, identify patterns, and uncover hidden customer segments that might not be immediately apparent.

- **Persona development:** It highlights the importance of creating detailed customer personas to guide sales efforts. The section explains how AI can help in creating accurate and comprehensive customer personas by analyzing data and identifying common traits, preferences, and behaviors among different customer groups.

3.3 Leveraging Data for Sales Intelligence:

- **Importance of data in sales intelligence:** This section emphasizes the role of data in driving sales intelligence and enabling smart selling decisions. It explains that data provides valuable insights into customer behavior, market trends, and sales performance, enabling sales teams to make informed decisions.

- **Types of data for sales:** The section discusses the various types of data that are relevant to sales, including customer data (demographic, behavioral, transactional), market data (competitor analysis, industry trends), and internal sales data (sales reports, CRM data).

- **AI-powered data analysis:** It explores how AI technologies can assist in data collection, integration, and analysis. The section highlights AI techniques such as data mining, machine learning algorithms, and predictive analytics, which can uncover patterns, trends, and correlations in sales data.

- **Data quality and governance:** The section addresses the importance of data quality and governance in leveraging data for smart selling. It emphasizes the need for accurate and reliable data, as well as proper data management practices to ensure data privacy, security, and compliance.

Chapter 3 provides comprehensive guidance on building a smart sales strategy. It covers setting clear sales goals and objectives, identifying target customers and segments, and leveraging data for sales intelligence. The chapter emphasizes the importance of aligning sales goals with business objectives, using AI to analyze data and gain insights into customer behavior, and employing data-driven strategies to enhance sales effectiveness. By incorporating these practices into their sales strategies, businesses can improve their targeting, engagement, and overall sales performance.

Chapter 4:

AI-Enabled Sales Techniques

4.1 Sales Automation and Workflow Optimization:

- **Introduction to sales automation:** This section explains the concept of sales automation and its role in streamlining sales processes. It highlights how AI technologies can automate repetitive and time-consuming tasks, allowing sales teams to focus on more strategic activities.

- **Identifying automation opportunities:** It discusses the steps involved in identifying tasks and processes that can be automated using AI. This includes analyzing sales workflows, identifying bottlenecks, and assessing the potential for efficiency gains through automation.

- **Implementing AI-powered automation:** The section explores different AI-powered tools and technologies that can be used for sales automation, such as AI chatbots, email automation, and CRM automation. It provides insights into how these tools can enhance sales efficiency, improve response times, and free up sales representatives' time for more value-added activities.

4.2 Personalization and Customer Experience Enhancement:

- **Importance of personalization in sales:** This section highlights the significance of personalization in creating a positive customer experience and driving sales success. It discusses how AI can enable personalization at scale by leveraging customer data and insights.

- **Utilizing AI for personalized recommendations:** It explores how AI can analyze customer data to generate personalized recommendations for products or services. This includes techniques like collaborative filtering, content-based filtering, and recommendation algorithms.

- **AI-powered customer journey mapping:** The section explains how AI can help in mapping and understanding the customer journey. It discusses the use of AI technologies to analyze customer interactions, predict customer behavior, and deliver personalized experiences at each touchpoint.

- **Enhancing customer engagement with AI:** It explores how AI-powered tools, such as chatbots and virtual assistants, can enhance customer engagement by providing personalized support, answering queries, and guiding customers through the sales process.

4.3 Predictive Lead Scoring and Qualification:

- **Introduction to predictive lead scoring:** This section explains the concept of predictive lead scoring and its importance in prioritizing and qualifying leads for sales teams. It discusses how AI algorithms can analyze data to predict lead quality and likelihood of conversion.

- **Data analysis for lead scoring:** It explores the types of data that can be used for lead scoring, such as demographic data, firmographic data, and behavioral data. The section discusses how AI can leverage this data to identify patterns and indicators of lead quality.

- **Implementing predictive lead scoring models:** The section outlines the steps involved in implementing predictive lead scoring models. This includes data preparation, model training, validation, and integration with CRM systems to provide real-time lead scoring and prioritization for sales teams.

4.4 Sales Forecasting and Pipeline Management:

- **Importance of sales forecasting:** This section highlights the significance of accurate sales forecasting in planning and decision-making. It explains how AI can contribute to more accurate and data-driven sales forecasting.

- **AI techniques for sales forecasting:** It discusses different AI techniques, such as time series analysis, regression models, and machine learning algorithms, that can be used for sales forecasting. The section explains how these techniques can analyze historical sales data, market trends, and external factors to predict future sales performance.

- **Managing sales pipelines with AI:** The section explores how AI can help in managing and optimizing sales pipelines. It discusses the use of AI-powered tools to track sales opportunities, analyze pipeline health, and identify areas for improvement. It also addresses how AI can provide sales teams with real-time insights and recommendations to prioritize and allocate resources effectively.

Chapter 4 focuses on AI-enabled sales techniques that can enhance sales effectiveness and improve customer experiences. It covers sales automation and workflow optimization, personalization and customer experience enhancement, predictive lead scoring and qualification, and sales forecasting and pipeline management. By leveraging AI in these areas, businesses can automate tasks, deliver personalized experiences, prioritize leads, and make more accurate sales forecasts, ultimately driving sales success and maximizing customer satisfaction.

Chapter 5:

Enhancing Sales with AI Tools

5.1 CRM and Sales Enablement Platforms:

- **Introduction to CRM:** This section provides an overview of Customer Relationship Management (CRM) systems and their role in sales. It explains how CRM platforms can centralize customer data, automate sales processes, and provide insights to enhance sales effectiveness.

- **Leveraging AI in CRM:** It explores how AI can enhance CRM capabilities, such as predictive analytics, lead scoring, and automated workflows. The section discusses how AI-powered CRM systems can improve sales forecasting, customer segmentation, and personalized customer engagement.

- **Implementing CRM and sales enablement platforms:** It outlines the steps involved in implementing CRM and sales enablement platforms. This includes data migration, customization, integration with other systems, and user training.

5.2 AI-Powered Sales Analytics and Reporting:

- **Importance of sales analytics:** This section emphasizes the value of sales analytics in driving data-driven decision-making. It explains how AI can analyze sales data to provide valuable insights and identify trends, patterns, and opportunities.

- **AI techniques for sales analytics:** It discusses various AI techniques, such as machine learning algorithms and natural language processing, that can be applied to sales analytics. The section explains how these techniques can uncover insights from structured and unstructured sales data, including CRM data, customer interactions, and market intelligence.

- **Generating AI-powered sales reports:** The section explores how AI can automate the generation of sales reports and dashboards. It discusses the benefits of real-time reporting, personalized dashboards, and visualizations that enable sales teams to track performance and make informed decisions.

5.3 Sales Chatbots and Virtual Assistants

- **Introduction to sales chatbots and virtual assistants:** This section explains how AI-powered chatbots and virtual assistants can enhance sales interactions and customer support. It discusses the advantages of using chatbots for lead qualification, product recommendations, and answering frequently asked questions.

- **Designing effective sales chatbots**: It explores the steps involved in designing and implementing sales chatbots. This includes defining chatbot objectives, creating conversational flows, training the chatbot with sales-related information, and continuous improvement based on customer interactions.

- **Virtual assistants for sales teams:** The section discusses how virtual assistants can assist sales teams by providing real-time insights, alerts, and recommendations. It explores how virtual assistants can improve sales productivity, streamline sales processes, and provide sales representatives with relevant information at their fingertips.

5.4 Voice and Speech Recognition in Sales

- **Voice technology in sales:** This section highlights the emerging role of voice and speech recognition in sales. It discusses how AI-powered voice assistants, such as Amazon Alexa or Google Assistant, can enable hands-free access to sales data, provide voice-activated reminders, and assist with sales-related tasks.

- **Voice analytics for sales:** It explores how AI can analyze voice interactions to extract valuable insights. The section discusses the use of natural language processing and sentiment analysis to understand customer preferences, identify sales opportunities, and personalize sales approaches.

- **Implementing voice and speech recognition:** The section provides insights into implementing voice and speech recognition technologies in sales, including integrating voice-enabled devices, ensuring data privacy and security, and optimizing the user experience.

Chapter 5 focuses on the utilization of AI tools in sales, including CRM platforms, sales analytics and reporting, sales chatbots and virtual assistants, and voice and speech recognition technologies. It explains the role of these tools in enhancing sales effectiveness, improving customer interactions, and providing valuable insights for decision-making. By leveraging AI in these areas, businesses can streamline sales processes, automate reporting, enhance customer engagement, and leverage voice-based technologies for hands-free sales support.

Chapter 6:

AI and Sales Performance Management

6.1 Sales Performance Metrics and KPIs:

- **Importance of sales performance metrics:** This section emphasizes the significance of tracking and measuring sales performance using relevant metrics and Key Performance Indicators (KPIs). It explains how metrics and KPIs provide insights into the effectiveness and efficiency of sales efforts.

- **AI-powered sales performance metrics:** It explores how AI can enhance sales performance measurement by automating data collection, analysis, and reporting. The section discusses how AI can provide real-time visibility into sales performance, identify trends, and generate predictive insights for proactive decision-making.

- **Choosing appropriate metrics and KPIs:** The section discusses the process of selecting metrics and KPIs that align with the sales objectives and business goals. It emphasizes the importance of selecting metrics that are measurable, actionable, and relevant to the sales team's activities and outcomes.

6.2 Sales Coaching and Training with AI:

- **Importance of sales coaching and training:** This section highlights the role of sales coaching and training in developing the skills and capabilities of sales representatives. It explains how continuous learning and improvement contribute to sales performance and success.

- **AI-powered sales coaching:** It explores how AI technologies can support sales coaching efforts. The section discusses AI-powered tools that provide personalized coaching recommendations, analyze sales conversations, and offer feedback on sales performance.

- **AI-driven sales training:** The section explores how AI can enhance sales training programs. It discusses the use of AI-powered virtual simulations, personalized training content, and adaptive learning platforms that cater to individual sales representatives' needs and learning styles.

6.3 AI-Driven Sales Incentive Programs:

- **Importance of sales incentives:** This section highlights the significance of sales incentives in motivating and rewarding sales teams. It explains how well-designed incentive programs can drive sales performance and align sales efforts with organizational objectives.

- **AI-enabled incentive program design:** It explores how AI can optimize sales incentive program design. The section discusses how AI algorithms can analyze sales data, individual performance, and market dynamics to recommend appropriate incentive structures, target-setting, and reward allocation.

- **Personalization in incentive programs:** The section emphasizes the value of personalization in sales incentive programs. It discusses how AI can help tailor incentives to individual sales representatives based on their performance, preferences, and goals.

6.4 Monitoring and Evaluating Sales Performance:

- **Importance of monitoring and evaluation:** This section explains the significance of monitoring and evaluating sales performance to track progress, identify areas for improvement, and drive continuous growth. It emphasizes the role of data analysis in assessing sales performance accurately.

- **AI-driven performance monitoring:** It explores how AI technologies can automate performance monitoring processes. The section discusses AI-powered tools that track and analyze sales data in real-time, generate performance dashboards, and provide actionable insights to sales managers and representatives.

- **Predictive analytics for sales performance:** The section explains how AI can leverage predictive analytics to forecast sales performance, identify potential challenges, and proactively address them. It explores how AI algorithms can analyze historical data, market trends, and external factors to generate forecasts and predictive insights.

Chapter 6 focuses on the integration of AI into sales performance management. It covers the importance of sales performance metrics and KPIs, the use of AI in sales coaching and training, AI-driven sales incentive programs, and the monitoring and evaluation of sales performance. By incorporating AI in these areas, businesses can gain real-time visibility into sales performance, enhance coaching and training programs, design effective incentive structures, and proactively monitor and improve sales performance based on data-driven insights.

Chapter 7:

Integrating AI into Sales Operations

7.1 Overcoming Challenges and Resistance to Change:

- **Introduction to challenges in AI integration:** This section discusses the common challenges and resistance that organizations may face when integrating AI into their sales operations. It explores factors such as lack of awareness, concerns about job displacement, and resistance from sales teams.

- **Addressing concerns and resistance:** It provides strategies for overcoming these challenges and addressing resistance to change. This includes fostering a culture of innovation and learning, providing proper training and support to sales teams, and transparently communicating the benefits of AI integration.

7.2 Implementing AI Solutions in Sales Teams:

- **Assessing AI readiness:** This section explains the importance of assessing the organization's readiness for AI integration. It discusses the need to evaluate factors such as data infrastructure, technical capabilities, and organizational alignment to ensure successful implementation.

- **Selecting appropriate AI solutions:** It explores the process of selecting AI solutions that align with the specific needs and objectives of the sales team. This includes considering factors such as functionality, scalability, integration capabilities, and vendor reputation.

- **Piloting and scaling AI implementation:** The section outlines the steps involved in piloting AI solutions within the sales team. It discusses the importance of starting small, measuring results, gathering feedback, and gradually scaling up the implementation based on success and lessons learned.

7.3 Data Privacy and Ethical Considerations in Smart Selling:

- **Importance of data privacy and ethics:** This section emphasizes the significance of data privacy and ethical considerations in the context of smart selling with AI. It explores the potential risks associated with data collection, storage, and usage, and the importance of maintaining customer trust.

- **Ensuring data privacy and security:** It discusses best practices for ensuring data privacy and security in AI-powered sales operations. This includes complying with relevant regulations (such as GDPR), implementing secure data storage and transfer protocols, and obtaining appropriate consent for data usage.

- **Ethical use of AI in sales:** The section addresses the ethical considerations in using AI for sales operations. It discusses the need for transparency, fairness, and accountability in AI algorithms and decision-making. It also explores the importance of addressing bias, ensuring inclusivity, and avoiding unethical practices in AI-enabled sales processes.

Chapter 7 focuses on integrating AI into sales operations. It covers overcoming challenges and resistance to change, implementing AI solutions in sales teams, and addressing data privacy and ethical considerations in smart selling. By addressing these aspects, businesses can successfully integrate AI into their sales operations, optimize sales processes, and ensure responsible and ethical use of AI technologies.

Chapter 8:

Case Studies: Real-World Examples of Smart Selling

8.1 AI Success Stories in B2B Sales:

- **Introduction to AI in B2B sales:** This section provides an overview of how AI has been successfully implemented in B2B sales processes. It discusses the benefits of AI in lead generation, lead scoring, customer segmentation, and personalized marketing strategies.

- **Case study examples:** It presents real-world case studies showcasing organizations that have effectively utilized AI in B2B sales. The section highlights specific AI tools and techniques used, such as predictive analytics, natural language processing, and CRM integration, and how they contributed to improved sales outcomes and customer experiences.

- **Key takeaways:** The section summarizes the key takeaways from the case studies, including the impact of AI on sales efficiency, revenue growth, and customer satisfaction in the B2B sales context.

8.2 AI-Driven Sales Strategies in E-commerce:

- **AI in e-commerce sales**: This section explores how AI has transformed sales strategies in the e-commerce industry. It discusses the use of AI-powered recommendation engines, personalized shopping experiences, chatbots, and virtual shopping assistants.

- **Case study examples:** It presents case studies of e-commerce companies that have successfully integrated AI into their sales strategies. The section highlights how AI has improved product recommendations, enhanced customer engagement, increased conversion rates, and streamlined the overall e-commerce sales process.

- **Lessons learned:** The section extracts key lessons learned from the case studies, such as the importance of data-driven personalization, seamless customer experiences across channels, and continuous optimization of AI algorithms to meet changing customer preferences.

8.3 Transforming Sales in Traditional Industries with AI:

- **AI adoption in traditional industries:** This section discusses how AI has disrupted and transformed sales processes in traditional industries, such as manufacturing, retail, and healthcare. It highlights the unique challenges faced by these industries and how AI solutions have addressed them.

- **Case study examples:** It presents real-world case studies of organizations in traditional industries that have successfully embraced AI in their sales operations. The section showcases how AI has improved demand forecasting, optimized inventory management, enhanced customer service, and increased sales revenue in these industries.

- **Key takeaways:** The section summarizes the key takeaways from the case studies, such as the importance of data integration, cross-functional collaboration, and change management when implementing AI in traditional industries.

8.4 Lessons Learned and Best Practices:

This section delves into the lessons learned and best practices from the case studies and real-world examples presented throughout the chapter. It highlights common themes and strategies that have emerged from successful implementations of AI in smart selling. These include the importance of having a clear vision and strategy for AI integration, fostering a culture of experimentation and learning, investing in robust data infrastructure and quality, and aligning AI initiatives with business goals and customer needs. Additionally, it emphasizes the significance of continuous monitoring, evaluation, and iteration to ensure ongoing optimization and improvement of AI-driven sales processes. By understanding these lessons and adopting best practices, organizations can navigate the complexities of integrating AI into their sales operations and drive sustainable growth and success.

By including this section on lessons learned and best practices, Chapter 8 provides valuable insights and guidance for organizations considering the implementation of AI in their sales strategies. It goes beyond showcasing individual case studies and synthesizes key takeaways and recommendations that can inform and guide the AI integration journey. These lessons and best practices serve as a roadmap for organizations to maximize the benefits of AI in smart selling while avoiding potential pitfalls and challenges.

Chapter 8 focuses on real-world case studies that highlight the successful implementation of AI in smart selling. It covers AI success stories in B2B sales, AI-driven sales strategies in e-commerce, and the transformation of sales in traditional industries with AI. By showcasing these case studies, the chapter provides concrete examples of how organizations across various sectors have leveraged AI to drive sales growth, improve customer experiences, and gain a competitive edge in the market.

Chapter 9:

The Future of Smart Selling

9.1 **Emerging Trends and Technologies in Sales:**

- This section explores the emerging trends and technologies that are shaping the future of smart selling. It discusses advancements such as augmented reality (AR) and virtual reality (VR) for immersive sales experiences, Internet of Things (IoT) for connected devices and data integration, and advanced analytics for predictive and prescriptive insights.

- **Adoption of intelligent automation:** It highlights the increasing adoption of intelligent automation in sales processes, including robotic process automation (RPA), AI-powered chatbots, and virtual assistants. The section explores how these technologies can streamline sales operations, automate repetitive tasks, and enable sales teams to focus on high-value activities.

- **Integration of voice and natural language processing:** It discusses the integration of voice recognition and natural language processing into sales interactions. The section explores how voice assistants and conversational AI can enhance customer engagement, enable voice-based ordering and support, and provide personalized recommendations.

9.2 **AI and the Future of Sales Roles and Skills:**

- **Evolution of sales roles:** This section delves into the evolving nature of sales roles due to AI integration. It discusses how AI technologies can automate routine tasks, freeing up sales professionals to focus on strategic relationship-building, complex problem-solving, and value-added activities.

- **Upskilling and reskilling:** It explores the importance of upskilling and reskilling sales teams to adapt to the changing landscape of smart selling. The section emphasizes the need for sales professionals to develop skills in data analysis, AI technologies, customer experience management, and consultative selling approaches.

- **Collaborative AI-human partnerships:** The section highlights the concept of collaborative AI-human partnerships, where AI technologies complement and augment the capabilities of sales professionals. It explores how sales teams can leverage AI tools as assistants and advisors, enhancing their productivity, efficiency, and decision-making.

9.3 Predictions for the Future of Smart Selling:

- **AI-driven personalization:** This section predicts that AI will continue to drive personalized sales experiences. It discusses how AI technologies can analyze vast amounts of customer data, preferences, and behaviors to deliver highly tailored product recommendations, pricing, and marketing messages.

- **Seamless omnichannel experiences:** It predicts that smart selling will enable seamless omnichannel experiences for customers. The section discusses how AI can integrate customer data across various touchpoints, enabling a consistent and personalized experience throughout the sales journey.

- **Enhanced sales forecasting and decision-making:** The section predicts that AI will continue to improve sales forecasting accuracy and support data-driven decision-making. It explores how AI-powered predictive analytics can identify trends, anticipate customer needs, and provide sales teams with actionable insights.

9.4 Ethical and Responsible AI in Sales:

- This section explores the growing importance of ethical and responsible AI practices in sales. It discusses the need for transparency, fairness, and accountability in AI algorithms and decision-making processes. The section emphasizes the ethical considerations in using AI for sales, such as ensuring the protection of customer data privacy, addressing bias and discrimination in AI models, and maintaining the trust and confidence of customers. It also discusses the role of organizations in establishing ethical guidelines and governance frameworks to guide the development and use of AI in sales operations.

9.5 Customer-Centric AI Solutions:

- This section focuses on the future of customer-centric AI solutions in smart selling. It discusses how AI technologies will enable organizations to gain deeper insights into customer preferences, behaviors, and needs. The section explores the potential for AI to enhance customer segmentation and targeting, deliver hyper-personalized recommendations, and provide proactive customer service. It also emphasizes the importance of leveraging AI to create seamless, frictionless customer experiences across multiple channels and touchpoints.

9.6 Collaboration between Humans and AI:

- This section delves into the concept of collaboration between humans and AI in smart selling. It discusses how AI technologies can augment the capabilities of sales professionals rather than replacing them. The section explores the potential for AI to assist in lead generation, customer engagement, and sales forecasting, while human sales professionals bring their unique insights, empathy, and relationship-building skills to the table. It emphasizes the need for organizations to foster a culture of collaboration and provide training and support to enable sales teams to effectively work alongside AI technologies.

- By addressing ethical considerations, focusing on customer-centric AI solutions, and promoting collaboration between humans and AI, Chapter 9 provides a holistic view of the future of smart selling. It emphasizes the importance of responsible AI practices, customer-centricity, and the symbiotic relationship between humans and AI. By embracing these principles and leveraging AI technologies strategically, organizations can shape the future of sales and drive meaningful business outcomes while prioritizing the needs and experiences of their customers.

Chapter 9 provides a glimpse into the future of smart selling by exploring emerging trends and technologies in sales, the evolution of sales roles and skills in the AI era, and predictions for the future of smart selling. By staying abreast of these developments, organizations can prepare for the future and leverage AI technologies to stay competitive, drive sales growth, and deliver exceptional customer experiences. The chapter emphasizes the importance of continuous learning, adaptation, and embracing the possibilities offered by AI to shape the future of sales.

Chapter 10:

Conclusion

The conclusion chapter serves as a summary of the key concepts discussed throughout the book and provides final thoughts on the topic of smart selling with AI.

1. Recap of Key Concepts:

- This section provides a concise recap of the main concepts, strategies, and technologies covered in the book. It highlights the importance of AI in transforming sales processes, improving customer experiences, and driving business growth.

- It revisits the key chapters and topics, such as AI-powered lead generation, personalized marketing, sales performance management, integrating AI into sales operations, real-world case studies, and predictions for the future of smart selling.

- The recap also emphasizes the significance of ethical considerations, customer-centricity, and collaboration between humans and AI in the context of smart selling.

2. Final Thoughts on Smart Selling with AI:

- This section offers the author's final thoughts and reflections on the subject matter. It may include insights on the current state of smart selling with AI and how organizations can leverage AI technologies to gain a competitive advantage.

- It may emphasize the ongoing evolution and dynamic nature of AI in sales and the need for continuous learning and adaptation.

- The final thoughts may also encourage readers to explore further resources and stay updated on the latest developments in AI and sales.

The conclusion chapter brings the book to a close, summarizing the main points discussed and providing a sense of closure to the topic of smart selling with AI. It aims to leave readers with a clear understanding of the benefits, challenges, and potential of integrating AI into sales processes and highlights the importance of responsible AI practices, customer-centricity, and collaboration between humans and AI. Ultimately, the conclusion chapter reinforces the message that AI is a powerful tool that, when used effectively and ethically, can revolutionize sales operations, enhance customer experiences, and drive business success in the increasingly digital and competitive marketplace.

The conclusion chapter also emphasizes the transformative impact of AI on sales professionals and organizations as a whole. It highlights how AI technologies have the potential to automate repetitive tasks, provide valuable insights and recommendations, and free up sales teams to focus on building relationships, providing strategic guidance, and delivering exceptional customer experiences. It encourages sales professionals to embrace the opportunities presented by AI and to continuously upskill and adapt their skills to thrive in the evolving landscape of smart selling.

Furthermore, the conclusion chapter underscores the importance of an iterative and learning mindset when implementing AI in sales operations. It acknowledges that the adoption of AI is a journey that requires continuous evaluation, refinement, and optimization. It encourages organizations to gather feedback, measure the impact of AI initiatives, and iterate on their strategies to ensure that they align with changing market dynamics, customer preferences, and technological advancements. By adopting a mindset of continuous improvement, organizations can maximize the benefits of AI and stay ahead of the competition.

Lastly, the conclusion chapter may also touch upon the broader societal implications of AI in sales. It acknowledges that while AI technologies offer immense potential for improving sales processes and customer experiences, they also raise important ethical and social considerations. It emphasizes the need for organizations to approach AI with responsibility, transparency, and accountability, ensuring that ethical guidelines and regulations are in place to protect customer privacy, prevent bias, and ensure fair and equitable treatment. By being mindful of these ethical considerations, organizations can harness the power of AI in a way that benefits not only their bottom line but also society as a whole.

In conclusion, the book has provided an in-depth exploration of smart selling with AI, covering various aspects such as lead generation, marketing, sales performance management, integration challenges, case studies, future trends, and ethical considerations. It has demonstrated the transformative potential of AI in sales and has equipped readers with the knowledge and insights needed to embrace AI technologies and drive sales success. By leveraging AI effectively, organizations can unlock new opportunities, optimize sales processes, and deliver exceptional value to customers in the dynamic and ever-evolving digital landscape.